P is for Puffin

A Newfoundland and Labrador Alphabet

Written by Janet Skirving and Illustrated by Odell Archibald

Sleeping Bear Press™
310 North Main Street, Suite 300
Chelsea, MI 48118
www.sleepingbearpress.com

© 2006 Sleeping Bear Press is an imprint of Gale, a part of Cengage Learning.

Printed and bound in China.

10 9 8 7 6 5 4 3 2

Library of Congress Cataloging-in-Publication Data

Skirving, Janet, 1963-
P is for puffin : a Newfoundland and Labrador alphabet / written by Janet
Skirving ; Illustrated by Odell Archibald.
p. cm.
Summary: "Newfoundland and Labrador's landscape, famous people, history,
and culture are introduced using the alphabet. Each letter's topic is introduced
with a simple poem. More detailed information on each topic is included in the
side-bar text"—Provided by publisher.
ISBN 978-1-58536-287-5 (alk. paper)
1. Newfoundland and Labrador—Juvenile literature. 2. English language—
Alphabet—Juvenile literature. I. Archibald, Odell, 1958- II. Title.
F1122.4.S45 2006
971.8—dc22   2006004302

In loving memory of my mother, Winnie.

To the other angels in my life, Jan Napier, Amy Lennex, and Heather Hughes
of Sleeping Bear Press, my deepest gratitude for your endless support.

A special thank you to Odell for your amazing talent in bringing this book to life.

JANET

Thank you to Sleeping Bear Press for the wonderful opportunity
to share this unique Newfoundland culture through my paintings.

To Lloyd Pretty for his patience and encouragement.
Thank you for bringing this beautiful world of art into my life.

To my husband Sandy for your constant support and encouragement.

And to my sons Stephen, Daniel, and Robert…my greatest achievements.

ODELL

There's a party going on.
Can you hear the music play?
People clapping, toes are tapping,
Accordion begins with A.

The people of Newfoundland and Labrador are very proud of their traditional music. It has a powerful and distinct sound. Songs like "I'se the B'y" and "Jack was every inch a Sailor" echo from the old countries like England, Ireland, and Scotland.

The accordion, often accompanied by the fiddle, is the backbone of the traditional sound. Today, the "jigs and reels" can be seen and heard anywhere from the kitchen and parlours to the concert stage.

During the annual folk festival in the summer of 2005, a record-breaking total of 989 musicians played their accordions simultaneously to the song "Mussels in the Corner." This feat entered them into the *Guinness Book of World Records*.

Many local musicians bring their own creativity through new songs. Groups such as Great Big Sea and the Irish Descendants are not only popular in Newfoundland and Labrador, they also entertain audiences all around the world.

Bb

B stands for Beothuks—
the first people of the land.
Brave hunters and gatherers who
were never afraid to take a stand.

Living in the central region, the Beothuks and their ancestors can be traced back more than 1,000 years. During the summer they lived on the coast where fish were plentiful. As winter approached they travelled inland following the Exploits River to the hunting grounds.

The Beothuks were Algonkian speaking and they called themselves "Red Indians." They painted their faces and bodies with a mixture of red ocre and grease. This was their mark of tribal identity and the very first coat was applied to their newborn babies. Described as trustworthy and proud, the Beothuks became extinct in 1829. The last known Beothuk was a young woman named Shanawdithit.

There are still several groups or bands of aboriginal people of Mi'kmaq origin scattered throughout western and central Newfoundland. In 1972 the Federation of Newfoundland Indians was officially formed.

Known along the Northern Peninsula as "Florence Nightingale of the North" Myra Bennett also begins with **B**. For 50 years she was the sole health provider for the entire isolated coast. Besides nursing, she practiced midwifery and dentistry.

Capelin is considered the main bait fish of the Arctic Seas. They move inshore to spawn or lay their eggs on the pebbly beaches. They attract and provide food for many seabirds, eagles, seals, and different species of whales during the summer. In Newfoundland the age-old tradition of scooping them up as they wash ashore is known as the capelin scull or capelin roll. During capelin season, people of all ages gather at the shorelines with dip nets and buckets. As the waves crash upon the beach, thousands of capelin are washed ashore. You have to be quick to fill your bucket before the waves pull them back in. Capelin are dried and salted and also enjoyed roasted over a campfire. Yum!!!

Confederation also begins with **C**. At midnight on March 31, 1949, Newfoundland and Labrador became the 10th province to join Canada, with Joseph R. Smallwood leading the campaign. Prior to this date, Newfoundland and Labrador was a British Colony.

Get your dip nets and buckets.
        The fish are rolling ashore.
C stands for Capelin.
        Let's go back and get some more!

What has webbed feet, a very strong tail,
and is an excellent swimmer at sea?
Always eager to learn and happy to please—
Newfoundland Dog becomes our D.

The Newfoundland dog, often referred to as "The Gentle Giant," is one of the largest dogs in the world. It can grow as tall as 71 centimetres and weigh nearly 70 kilograms.

This dog is intelligent, a fast learner, and best known for its swimming and life-saving skills. They were traditionally used for tracking and pulling heavy carts. They were also found at sea helping fishermen. The dogs would fetch anything that fell overboard and help pull in the heavy nets filled with fish. If a fisherman fell overboard, the dog would save him.

Another dog that was equally as helpful and loyal was the Labrador retriever or sometimes referred to as the St. John's dog. This smaller breed was invaluable to hunters because of its incredible sense of smell.

Downhill skiing also begins with **D** and is a very popular winter sport. Marble Mountain Ski Resort with an elevation of nearly 550 metres is the largest in Atlantic Canada and is situated in Steady Brook on Newfoundland's west coast.

Dd

Ee

This famous pirate ruled the seas
with many sailors under his power.
Peter Easton stands for E.
He plundered ships in the darkest hours.

When Peter Easton first arrived in Newfoundland in 1602 he was a loyal English seaman and officer. The following year when the battles with Spain slowed down, the English Navy dissolved and Peter Easton became a pirate! With thousands of sailors under his control he plundered ships and raided harbours for the next 20 years. He captured many treasures and fortunes. Many stories are still told today of these treasures and where they are hidden. Could this be true?

This swashbuckling pirate set up headquarters in Harbour Grace in 1610. As pirates are highly mobile, Peter Easton moved further south to Ferryland, also on the Avalon Peninsula, where he stayed until 1614.

During his reign, many ships were dispatched from England and France in hopes of capturing the "Pirate Admiral" and bringing justice and stability to the people. He was never captured! Peter Easton retired in France and became the "Marquis of Savoy." He lived the rest of his life in great luxury!

Newfoundland and Labrador has had several flags in the past. As a British Colony we flew the Union Jack. Labradorians are proud of their own flag with the spruce twig in the upper left corner. Many Newfoundlanders remain loyal to their native flag of pink, white, and green, which originated in 1843. The official provincial flag, however, was adopted in 1980 and flown for the first time on Discovery Day, June 24 of the same year.

Our flag was designed by Newfoundland artist Christopher Pratt. The blue represents the sea. The white symbolizes snow and ice. The red stands for human effort, and the gold represents the confidence we have in ourselves and our future. The design of the provincial flag symbolizes the past, present, and future of our province.

Ff

First flown on Discovery Day, the people were proud to show the official Flag that begins with F as it waved to and fro.

G stands for Gros Morne—
a famous national park.
With all its natural beauty,
it has certainly left its mark.

Gros Morne National Park, situated on the west coast of Newfoundland, was designated a UNESCO World Heritage Site in 1987. Long Range Mountains, waterfalls, and wildlife are just part of its beauty. The most unique features of Gros Morne are its towering rock formations and freshwater fjords.

It has been reported that in the 1700s British warships stopped at Gros Morne to rest. In the 1800s sportsmen arrived to hunt and fish. The years following brought adventurers, naturalists, photographers, and geologists.

Newfoundland's other national park is Terra Nova National Park. It is situated in central Newfoundland. This 400 square kilometre park includes coniferous forests and a rugged coastline with many ponds and streams in between.

The "Crossroads of the World," Gander International Airport also begins with **G**. In the 1940s it was considered the world's largest airport. Gander airport played a vital role during and after WWII, since a fuel stop was a necessity for all flights travelling overseas.

Gg

H is for Mina Hubbard.
Like her husband who tried before,
she set out on an expedition
to map the interior of Labrador.

H h

It was a century ago that Mina Hubbard set out to map the interior of Labrador. Her husband Leonidas had made the attempt two years earlier, but died during his effort. In honour of her husband, Mina set out in 1905 to finish what he had set out to do. This time, however, Mina had another goal! She challenged her husband's former partner Dillon Wallace to a race. She completed the trek through Labrador, and in fact, finished the expedition a month and a half before Wallace.

Considering the harsh environment and rugged landscape, it was truly remarkable for a woman to take on such a mission. Not only did Mina complete the first accurate map of the river system in Labrador, but she proved to be one of the finest explorers and cartographers of her time.

Ii

Icebergs break away from glaciers
and they begin with the letter I.
See them drift down Iceberg Alley
and tower high into the sky.

Icebergs are formed as they break away or "calve off" from glaciers. It takes an iceberg one to two years to drift southward from Western Greenland into Iceberg Alley. This alley is situated along the eastern coastal waters of Newfoundland and Labrador. Although icebergs float in the salty Atlantic Ocean, they are actually formed from freshwater glaciers. A large iceberg may tower as high as 75 metres, but the amazing fact is that seven-eighths of the iceberg rests below the waterline.

Did you know that the word *iceberg* comes from ijsberg, which is Dutch for "ice hill?"

I also stands for Innu and Inuit which are two of the aboriginal groups living in Labrador. The third group is the Metis. The Inuit are descendants of the Thule people who came from the Canadian Arctic some 800 years ago. The Innu, formerly known as the Naskapi-Montagnais, were living in Labrador when the Europeans arrived. The Metis are descendants of both the Europeans and the Inuit people. The term *Metis* means mixed.

In the old downtown streets of St. John's, the capital of Newfoundland, you will find many wooden houses built in a row. They are joined together and share one common wall. What stands out the most among these row houses is that they are painted in bright, vivid colours of red, blue, green, and even purple! These beautifully decorated houses line the streets and have caught the attention of many visitors over the years. These streets of multicoloured houses have been nicknamed Jelly Bean Row.

Why the bright colours, you ask? Like the people and culture of the province, the homes are bright, colourful, and cheery!

Jj

J stands for Jelly Bean Row.
What a funny name. Do you know why?
These colourful houses line the streets,
and they will certainly catch your eye!

The people of Labrador have survived very harsh climates for centuries. During the winter months when it was necessary to travel over ice and snow, the Inuit people used dogsleds or, as they called them, komatiks. These komatiks were led by teams of a few or many dogs depending on the load to be carried. They were used to carry people, wood, supplies, or carry game home from a hunt. In later years komatiks were used to carry mail during the winter.

The traditional komatik ranged from almost three to four metres in length and was wrapped in animal hides such as sealskin and bear. The hunter or racer would sit or lie down, facing forward as the dogs whisked him away.

The husky is the most commonly used sled dog. They are strong and energetic with a thick coat to protect them from the extreme temperatures.

The Inuit word is Komatik.
This dogsled begins with K.
It races over ice and snow.
Hurray, get out of its way!

Lighthouse begins with L,
    each one built as a mariner's aid.
With bright lights and looming towers,
    they ensured a safe voyage was made.

Lighthouses scattered along the coastline of Newfoundland and Labrador have been in operation for almost 200 years. The first was built at Fort Amherst at the mouth of the St. John's harbour in 1813, where a lighthouse still stands today. These towers were built to either safely guide mariners to land or warn them of approaching land.

Traditionally, lighthouses were simple structures with lanterns or lamps which were lit at night to guide the ships at sea. They were manned by a lighthouse keeper. Many years later the keepers would be responsible for an entire light station, which included not only the lighthouse itself but the fog signal building, the radio beacon equipment, and the keeper's dwelling. Many lighthouses remain today, but most are controlled and maintained by the Canadian Coast Guard.

In 1919 Captain John Alcock and Lieutenant Arthur Whitten Brown took off on the first nonstop transatlantic flight from Lester's Field, which also begins with **L**. Fifteen hours and 57 minutes later the two pilots landed in Clifton, Ireland. What an adventure!

Ll

M is for Mummers.
It's a Christmas tradition
when the neighbours come knocking
and enter your kitchen.

M m

The tradition of mummering was brought to the island with the arrival of its original Irish and English settlers. Today in many rural areas this tradition lives on.

The mummers dress up or "janny up" in old, worn clothing. They stuff their clothes with pillows, cover their faces with masks or veils, and even disguise their voices. These wanderers roam from house to house spreading laughter, cheer, and sometimes a little mischief. Once their identity has been revealed, they entertain the host with some traditional music and dance, enjoy some Christmas treats, and then move on to the next house!

Marystown also begins with **M**. Situated on the Burin Peninsula, it's known around the world for its shipyard. The Marystown Shipyard built many fishing vessels and several tugs. In the 1970s it began building offshore oil vessels as interest began to shift to the oil industry. Today the shipyard is very active in the retrofitting and servicing of offshore oil rigs.

On June 29, 1898, Newfoundland's very first express train steamed out of St. John's and arrived in Port aux Basques on the west coast more than 27 hours later.

Why was it called the "Newfie Bullet" you ask? Although this locomotive was known for its great quality and service, its lack of speed quickly became obvious. The train jokingly became known by its nickname.

The Newfie Bullet encountered many unique challenges over the years. The island had a narrow gauge track, which meant the tracks were not as wide as those used on the mainland. Every train arriving in the province by ship had to readjust its wheels in order to fit the narrow tracks on the island. Deep snow-drifts would stop the train for days and winds have been known to blow the train off the tracks. When the Trans Canada Highway was completed, changes took place and fewer passengers travelled by train. July 3, 1969, marked the last official journey of the Newfie Bullet.

The Newfie Bullet begins with N.
You would think this train was fast
but if ever it was in a race,
it would certainly come in last!

These communities nestle along the coast.
It's where the first settlers would go
to start a new life and live off the sea.
Outports begin with O.

A few hundred years ago when the first inhabitants arrived from England and Ireland, they settled in outports or coastal communities. The Atlantic Ocean would be their livelihood. It made perfect sense to establish their homes, churches, boats, and wharves along the coastline. Travel was done by boat from one community to the next.

When the railway began in the 1890s, communities began to crop up in the interior of the province and the construction of roads began. After Confederation, the residents of the outports were strongly encouraged to resettle in the larger communities where more services were available to them, such as schools and health care. Their lives were already established and had been for many years. It was a difficult decision to make.

Although fewer people live in the outports today, many descendants of the first settlers still remain. The outports are still the heart and soul of Newfoundland and Labrador. These communities represent our history and have helped to mold the culture we have today.

P p

It's a funny little seabird—
Puffin begins with **P**.
Coloured orange, yellow, and blue,
and called the Clown of the Sea.

The Atlantic Puffin with its multicoloured beak and bright orange feet was named the official bird in 1992. When at sea, puffins fly, float, and even dive underwater for fish. They can withstand the freezing Arctic waters because they have thick layers of fat to keep them warm and coats of airtight and water repellent feathers.

Witless Bay Ecological Reserve is a beautiful spot for watching these funny seabirds at play in their own natural habitat.

P also stands for pitcher plant. The provincial flower grows only a few inches tall. It is a carnivorous or meat-eating plant but only a threat to insects! The bugs are attracted to the bright red and green leaves and if they dare to enter, there is no escape. The native people used the roots of the plant for medicine to treat stomach cramps, tuberculosis, smallpox, and fever. The pitcher plants are mostly found in bogs and marshland.

Quidi Vidi Battery (pronounced *Kitty Viddy*) is a provincial historic site. The Battery or site of the artillery unit was first built in June, 1762 by the French. They had taken control of St. John's and the Quidi Vidi Battery was built to defend themselves against a counter-attack. Their control of St. John's would last only a few months. The British, led by Lieutenant Colonel William Amherst regained control three months later. The Battery was rebuilt and expanded several times throughout the years. On many occasions it served as a protector for St. John's.

Today, Quidi Vidi provincial historic site is open to the public. Visitors can learn all about the history of the Battery from interpreters who dress in military uniforms from that period. These inter-preters also reenact the activities carried out by the soldiers who guarded the city many years ago.

An important part of our history
Quidi Vidi Battery begins with Q.
Overlooking the village below,
built by the French in 1762.

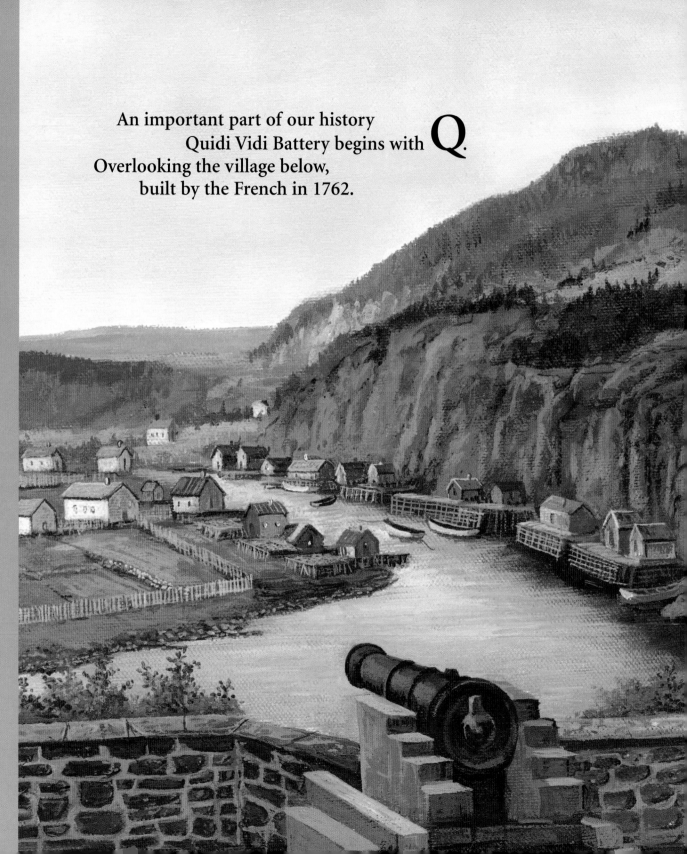

The Royal Regatta begins with **R**.
It's when the annual event takes place.
The rowers are lined up and ready.
Who will win the race?

The oldest ongoing sporting event in North America, the Royal St. John's Regatta, takes place on the first Wednesday of August on Quidi Vidi Lake. The first event took place in September of 1818.

Each boat or shell has a crew of six plus one coxswain. Both men and women compete and the ages range from 14 years old to senior citizens. Live music streams from the bandstand, and the lake is surrounded by a variety of food and fun. There are games of chance, skill, raffles, and toys to be won!

There are two other annual regattas which take place on the island. Since 1862 Harbour Grace has held their own regatta on Lady Lake. In 1963 Placentia hosted its first annual day at the races. The highest honour of all is called the Triple Crown. This award goes to the rowing team who places first in all three regattas.

R r

The oldest city in North America
with a culture all of its own,
Stands for St. John's,
The place we call "Downhome."

St. John's is the capital of Newfoundland and Labrador and the oldest city in North America. It was discovered in 1497 by John Cabot and sits on the eastern edge of Canada. St. John's became world renowned because of its abundance of fish. Ships sailed from all over the world to reap the rewards.

Our capital is built around a protected harbour, and ships must sail through a narrow gap to enter. Approaching the "Narrows" from the outside, ships are confronted with a solid wall of cliffs until the entrance of the harbour finally appears!

High above the harbour is Signal Hill, where Guglielmo Marconi received the first transatlantic wireless message in Morse code in 1901 sent from Cornwall, England .

Today St. John's is a modern, bustling city, yet its uniqueness continues to surround you. The very air you breathe tastes of salt and it's a great city to get lost in. There are many steep hills to climb, narrow alleyways to explore, and tasty dishes to try.

Toutons are made from leftover bread dough, formed into little patties, pan-fried until golden brown, and then drizzled with molasses. Yum! They are just one of the authentic tastes that you will experience in Newfoundland and Labrador. How about a "good feed" of salt fish and brewis served with scrunchins or fatback pork?

Would you like to try cod tongues or jigg's dinner with pease pudding? There are so many choices on the menu. Care to try some flipper pie, moose stew, or caribou? Save room for dessert because we have bakeapple cheesecake and partridgeberry pie. Perhaps you would prefer our Figgy Duff which is a sixteenth century traditional steamed pudding.

What a feast, or as we say, "What a scoff!"

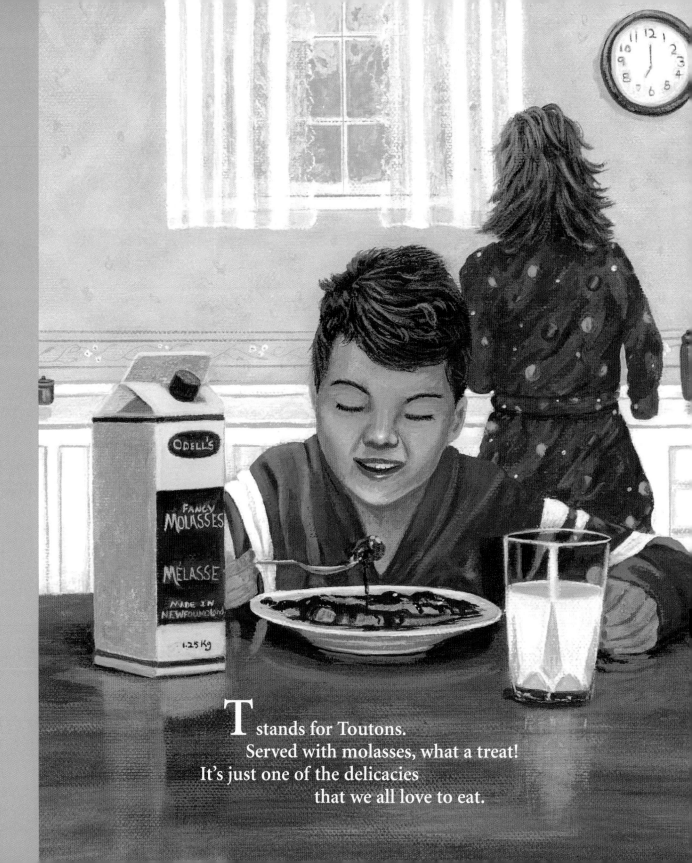

T t

T stands for Toutons.
Served with molasses, what a treat!
It's just one of the delicacies
that we all love to eat.

U u

Can you follow the beat of the music?
Any instrument will do.
It really doesn't matter
even an Ugly stick that begins with U.

When a party breaks out in the province, a good time is had by all. Traditional music has been deeply rooted in the culture for hundreds of years. You will find many different instruments here; accordions, fiddles, harmonicas, spoons, and yes, even ugly sticks!

Each ugly stick is unique and each one is homemade. The only thing that they all have in common is the harsh sounding noise that they create. To use the ugly stick, you simply tap it on the floor to the beat of the music.

Creating your own ugly stick is easy. With a long stick or a mop, you nail an old boot or shoe to the bottom. At the top of the stick you can nail an empty tin can or bottle caps. You then attach anything at all that makes a rattling noise. You can be as creative as you like. There's only one rule; have fun!

V

Records show that around 1000 A.D., while exploring the Labrador coast, the Vikings founded and settled in L'Anse aux Meadows, which is located on the northeast coast of Newfoundland. The expedition was led by Leif Erickson and his crew. The Vikings soon realized the fish were plentiful, the wooded area would provide timber for their homes and boats, and the vast open meadows would be ideal for their livestock.

It was many centuries later, in 1960, that a Norwegian explorer and writer, Helge Ingstad, discovered the old Viking colony. The overgrown bumps and ridges found in L'Anse aux Meadows proved to be the remains of the Old Norse buildings from the eleventh century. It was at this point that the excavation began.

L'Anse aux Meadows was designated a National Historic Site in 1977, and in the following year it was recognized as the only Viking site in North America and declared a UNESCO World Heritage Site.

As their ships sailed the great seas
one thousand years ago,
the Vikings, which begin with V,
settled in L'Anse aux Meadows.

Whales begin with **W.**
       There are many species to be found.
Orca, Pilot, or Humpback—
       Can you tell by the sound?

Sightings of humpback, pilot or minke whales are quite common, but to spot an orca is truly a rare occurrence. The orca is the largest member of the dolphin family. From early spring until late fall, Newfoundland and Labrador is home to 22 species of whales. The whales spend their winters in the south where the waters are warm. In the spring, they venture north along the Atlantic coast where the rich marine life becomes their summer feeding ground.

Every whale has a unique vocalization or sound. The pilot whale is the noisiest of all, with a variety of clicks and whistles. If you get close enough, you can hear them.

There are many ways to go whale watching in the province. A boat tour can bring you so close it will take your breath away! With the help of binoculars, you can clearly see the incredible mammals right from the shoreline. From many miles away you can see them "breaching," or thrusting their bodies out of the water and splashing into the ocean again. What a thrill!

According to maritime research, there are hundreds of shipwrecks surrounding Newfoundland and Labrador. These records include the last two centuries alone. The most renowned shipwreck is the *Titanic*. On the night of April 15 1912, the ship sank after hitting an iceberg 523 kilometres southeast off the Newfoundland coast. The disaster claimed the lives of more than 1,500 passengers and crew.

There are many causes of shipwrecks. A ship may sink if caught in a hurricane, snow storm, strong currents, or tidal waves. Like the *Titanic*, ships could run into icebergs or may become disoriented by dense fog and run ashore. Human error could also be a factor. A ship may be poorly built. The captain's skills of seamanship may be challenged. The ship may have been taken over by pirates or its own shipmates, as in a mutiny. The reasons are endless. If these ships and sailing vessels could talk, what a tale they would tell!

At the bottom of the ocean
lay many shipwrecks.
You can find them on the map;
they are marked with an X!

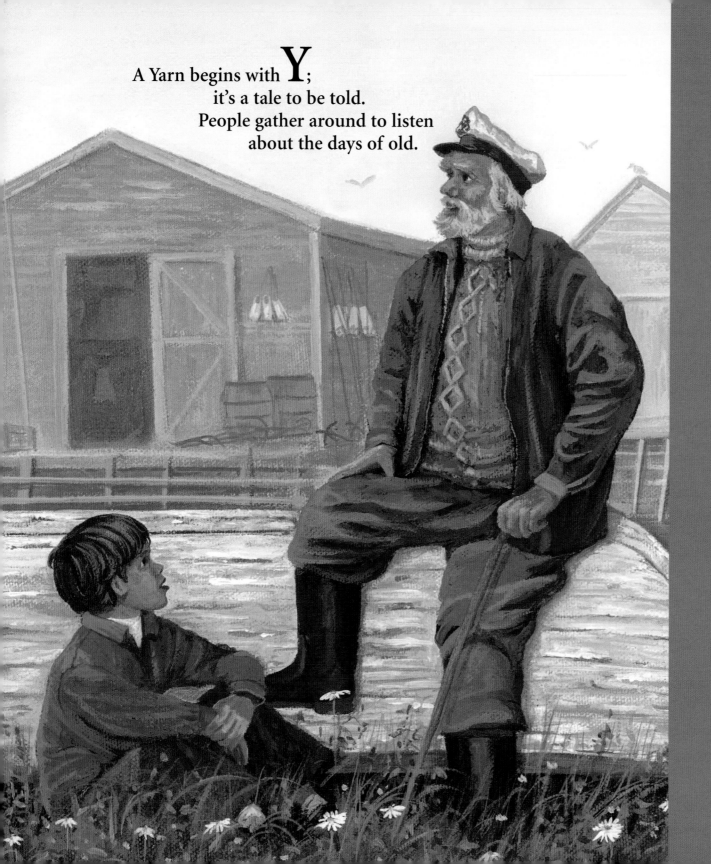

A Yarn begins with **Y**;
it's a tale to be told.
People gather around to listen
about the days of old.

Yy

Storytelling or a good "yarn" has always been a very important part of our rich traditional heritage. You can even hear some of these stories in our songs.

Our province remained isolated for many years, especially in the outports. There was no electricity, certainly no television as there is today. Story-telling was a great source of entertainment. It was mostly in the home where the greatest yarns and songs were shared and passed down from the elders. Today a good old yarn told in our own dialect is still a special treat to hear.

Our English is similar to that of southeast Ireland where many of our ancestors originated. Mix this Irish accent with that of England and Scotland and you will hear the unique accent that we have today. Being so isolated for centuries, we were able to retain it. We even have our own *Dictionary of Newfoundland English*. If you visit Newfoundland and Labrador, you will hear many different expressions like:

How ya gettin'on, b'y? — How are you?
Awful nice day! — What a beautiful day!
Where you 'longs to? — Where are you from?

Z stands for Time Zone.
It's unique on the "Rock."
  When the world is on the hour,
  it's half past on our clock!

Why is Newfoundland time unique? Whereas the other provinces lie within a time zone, Newfoundland rests on a dividing line of a time zone, making it halfway between two time zones—that is to say, that if it's 12:00 in Nova Scotia, it's 12:30 in Newfoundland.

As it is throughout the world, Canada is divided into time zones. There are a total of six in the country; Newfoundland time zone, Atlantic, Eastern, Central, Mountain, and Pacific time. The Earth is divided into many lines of longitude and our time zones follow, more or less, these lines or meridians.

Is Labrador on Newfoundland or Atlantic time? Both, depending on your location. If you are south of the community of Cartwright, you are on Newfoundland time. If you are north of Cartwright, you are on Atlantic time.

Time zones were created by a Canadian, Sir Sanford Fleming. On November 18, 1883, standard time was introduced in North America.

z Z

Lighthouse Full of Learning

1. Name some of the musical instruments heard in Newfoundland and Labrador.
2. Why were the Beothuks known as the "Red Indians?"
3. When did Newfoundland join Confederation?
4. Who was "Florence Nightingale of the North?"
5. Who was the famous pirate who plundered ships and raided harbours?
6. Where is the "Crossroads of the World?"
7. Where do icebergs come from?
8. Do you know how iceberg got its name?
9. Can you name the three aboriginal groups living in Labrador?
10. What is Jelly Bean Row?
11. What is a Komatik?
12. What is the purpose of a lighthouse?
13. What are Mummers?
14. What is the "Newfie Bullet?"
15. What is the "Clown of the Sea?"
16. When was the first Royal Regatta?"
17. Who was Mina Hubbard?
18. What is the capital of Newfoundland and Labrador?
19. What is the name of the largest ski resort in Atlantic Canada?
20. Where did the Vikings first settle over 1,000 years ago?
21. Can you name some of the whale species found in Newfoundland and Labrador?
22. Who created the time zone?
23. Can you name some of the traditional meals served in Newfoundland and Labrador?
24. How do you make an ugly stick?

Answers

1. Accordion, fiddle, spoons, harmonica, and ugly stick
2. They painted their faces and bodies with a mixture of red ocre and grease.
3. At midnight on March 31, 1949
4. Myra Bennett
5. Peter Easton
6. Gander International Airport
7. They are formed as they break away from glaciers.
8. From the Dutch word "ijsberg," which means ice hill.
9. Innu, Inuit, and Metis
10. A streetful of bright and colourful row houses
11. An Inuit word for a dog sled
12. To safely guide mariners to land or warn them of approaching land.
13. People who dress up in silly disguises and wander from house to house entertaining the hosts.
14. The famous train that serviced Newfoundland for many years.
15. The provincial bird, the puffin
16. September, 1818
17. She was the famous cartographer who mapped the interior of Labrador.
18. St. John's
19. Marble Mountain
20. L'Anse aux Meadows
21. Humpback, pilot, minke, finback and orca
22. Sir Sanford Fleming
23. Fish and Brewis with scrunchins, cod tongues, jigg's dinner, flipper pie and moose stew to name a few
24. Nail an old boot or shoe to the bottom of a mop or long stick, attach some bottle caps, tin cans, or anything that makes a rattling noise

Janet Skirving

Janet Skirving was born and raised in St. John's, Newfoundland. She is the youngest of three daughters, and completed all of her schooling on the island including studies at Memorial University of Newfoundland. Janet graduated in 1987 with a Bachelor of Arts degree in French and English Literature.

Growing up on the island she quickly developed the travel bug and has always been fascinated with different cultures and languages. She began her career as a flight attendant in 1988 and now, many years later, still thoroughly enjoys the path she has chosen.

Odell Archibald

Odell (Trask) Archibald grew up in the small town of Stephenville Crossing in Newfoundland and is the youngest of eleven children. She paints almost daily, drawing inspiration and ideas from her familiar surroundings and personal memories. Although relatively new to the fine art scene, she captures simple, timeless moments in her art using her unique style of realism. Her love for family and country living is reflected in her work.

Odell has lived on the south coast in Burgeo and Burin. She has come to appreciate and love the outport community lifestyle. She now resides in Kippens with her husband and has three sons. She enjoys hiking, canoeing and spends most weekends at her cottage on a beautiful Salmon River in western Newfoundland.